FREESTYLE MOTOCROSS
JUMP TRICKS FROM THE PROS

GARTH MILAN

MBI Publishing Company

DEDICATION

This book is dedicated to the love of my life, Sylvia Gonzales, and my parents for their loving support and constant contributions.

WARNING

Freestyle motocross is an extremely dangerous and sometimes fatal sport. All riders pictured in this book are professionals using proper protective gear under controlled conditions. This book should not and does not serve as an instructional manual, but is an explanation of how riders perform insane freestyle motocross moves. Attempting to duplicate any of the maneuvers may be hazardous and/or fatal and is not recommended. Readers are cautioned that individual abilities, motorcycles, terrain, jumps, and riding conditions differ, and due to these unlimited factors beyond the control of the authors and riders quoted in this book, liability is expressly disclaimed. Do not attempt any maneuvers, stunts, or techniques that are beyond your capabilities.

First published in 2000 by MBI Publishing Company, 729 Prospect Avenue, PO Box 1, Osceola, WI 54020-0001 USA

© Garth Milan, 2000

MBI Publishing Company books are also available at discounts in bulk quantity for industrial or sales-promotional use. For details write to Special Sales Manager at Motorbooks International Wholesalers & Distributors, 729 Prospect Avenue, PO Box 1, Osceola, WI 54020-0001 USA

Library of Congress Cataloging-in-Publication Data
Milan, Garth
    Freestyle motocross: jump tricks from the pros / Garth Milan.
        p. cm.
    Includes index
    ISBN 0-7603-0926-4 (pbk. : alk. paper)
        1. Motocross. I. Title.

GV1060.12.M55 2000
796.7'56–dc21   00-033918

On the front cover: Mike Metzger, Cliffhanger; Insets: Ronnie Faisst, Nac-Nac.

On the frontispiece: From top: Travis Pastrana, Indian Air Superman Seat Grab; Ronnie Faisst, Cordova; Kris Garwasiuk, Bar Hop; Trevor Vines, Double Can-Can.

On the title page: Left: Mike Craig, Whip. Right: Clifford Adoptante, Indian Air Superman Seat Grab.

On the index page: Kris Rourke, Whip.

On the back cover: Clifford Adoptante, Stalefish Saran Wrap; Inset: Reagan Sieg, Hart Attack.

Edited by Sara Perfetti
Layout by Tom Heffron

Printed in China

CONTENTS

ACKNOWLEDGMENTS

Writing this book would never have been possible without the help of some very inspirational people. First on the list is Ken Faught from *Dirt Rider* magazine, who basically began my career as a photojournalist in the great sport of motocross. Thanks for giving a young "kid" like me a chance to contribute to the activity I love. Next is Wayne Kelly, who provided me with tons of wisdom about photography and pushed me well beyond the limits I previously thought existed in me.

Lee Klancher from MBI Publishing Company also gets my thanks for providing me with the opportunity to publish a book about an exciting new sport that really deserves some good exposure.

My family definitely should receive some recognition as well. To start with, my brother Bret, who introduced me to motorcycles in the first place, way back in 1987. And next, my parents, who gave me the support and encouragement to chase not only my motocross dreams, but also my scholastic goals, which led to a bachelor of science degree in photojournalism from California State University, Long Beach.

A special thanks is also extended to the riders who contributed so much to the production of this book: Kris Rourke, Ronnie Faisst, Mike Metzger, Brian Deegan, and Larry Linkogle.

— Garth Milan

Author Garth Milan is no stranger to the freestyle scene. Milan is the assistant editor of *TransWorld Motocross* and has freelanced for several different advertising clients and publications in the motocross industry.

by Mike Metzger

Freestyle motocross is my way of life. Motorcycles have always been part of my existence, since the day I was born. My dad rode me around on his dirt bikes until he bought me my own Suzuki JR50 when I was three years old. My only goals growing up were to win races and eventually get a factory ride as a professional racer. Unfortunately, being healthy and in shape is an important aspect of being a pro in the sport of motocross.

From the time I was very young until now, I have been plagued with constant injuries in every sport I have tried. Motorcycle riding just seems to be the sport I have always been drawn back to. Even after breaking both femurs, along

with at least a dozen other big bones and countless smaller ones, the rush from riding a dirt bike is equal to none.

The word "free" to me means no rules or boundaries. When I ride my motorcycle and get away from everyday business life, it is the only stress reliever that makes me truly feel free, in the fullest sense of the word. To me, the best feeling of getting away is taking a trip to the desert with my freeride buddies and cruising across God's landscape. The power of a two-stroke beneath me is a sensation that I honestly can't describe. All I can say is that if you want to know the feeling, make sure your prayers are said and that Jesus Christ is riding with you.

My plans for the future of freestyle and freeride motocross include innovating new motorcycle parts and accessories, building bigger ramps, designing more technical courses, producing better safety protection, working with the riders, getting more corporate sponsors involved, and simply making the sport as big as humanly possible. I feel that the motorcycle freeride industry has tons of room to expand and to allow new ideas to form, and books like this are exactly what we need to really blow up the sport and show everyone just how awesome freestyle is and how big we go.

With the increased exposure from this book and televised extreme sports contests on network television running weekly programs on motocross, the public is able to form an opinion on our sport. Good or bad, those opinions travel throughout the minds of adventurous humans in this world who want to try something new. I hope that, by reading this book and seeing us at contests and on television, the new hobby chosen by those adrenaline junkies will be the great sport of freestyle motocross. So remember, always wear your safety gear, ride at your own risk, and God Bless.

HOLD IT WIDE!!!

METZGER 7

INTRODUCTION AND HISTORY OF THE SPORT

Competitive motorcycle racing has been around for over half a century, but with a new millennium upon us there is a fresh group of young athletes taking the sport to a thrilling new direction with more excitement than ever before. Freestyle motocross has captured the attention of the motorcycle world like nothing in recent history and is growing by leaps and bounds every year. The sport is basically a spin-off of traditional off-road motorcycle riding; but instead of banging elbows with a pack of other riders while hitting berms and whoops, riders compete by launching themselves over huge gaps where they pull off a variety of freestyle tricks.

This may not look a lot like modern freestyle, and it's not, but it does show a big part of freestyle's heritage. Many riders, including Mike Metzger, started off by doing slow-speed foot plants. Although it might not look difficult, a rider can snap a femur just the same as if he were to come up short on a 100-foot gap.

Jeremy McGrath's Nac-Nac grabbed a lot of attention when he started pulling them in stick and ball stadiums in the mid-1990s. McGrath is one of the founding fathers of freestyle, even though he's never competed in a true freestyle event.

Whether a rider is fairly new to the sport and just learning how to jump, or is preparing to compete in some of the increasingly popular events held in stadiums across the country, the feelings experienced are the same. Anyone who has ever launched a motorcycle into the air knows how wonderful it feels being at the edge of control, pushing past limits that were previously thought to be impenetrable, and coming back safely.

The principle behind this book is to provide readers with an illustration of the tricks that freestylers are executing, and to give riders a chance to explain how they pull off such maneuvers. A photo gallery is also included to give the reader a behind-the-scenes look at what the sport is all about.

Riders like Mike Metzger, Larry Linkogle, Ronnie Faisst, Brian Deegan, and Kris Rourke are just a few of the talented professionals who have taken time out of their busy schedules to lend their expertise and personal techniques to this book.

A History of Freestyle Motocross

Although organized freestyle competitions have been around for only a few short years, doing tricks on off-road motorcycles is not a new concept. In the 1980s, such Supercross stars as David Bailey and Rick Johnson celebrated their victories by doing tricks such as No-Handers (taking both hands off the handlebars in midair). What is new, however, is the concept

Mike Metzger's Double Can-Can was considered radical in 1996, but compared to the Switchblades he is doing now, it looks pretty tame. Extension of moves is one of the many changes that the sport has seen in its infant years.

One of the greatest tricksters of all time is Guy Cooper. Even though he was an AMA 125-cc National Champion, he was more famous for the big whips and wild antics he pulled at races all over the world than he was for his track speed. He's also one of the first riders who jumped big gaps to impress his friends instead of television audiences.

of an event where the riders compete strictly by doing these crowd-pleasing tricks rather than racing to the finish line. This idea was bred by the fact that despite the excitement of motocross and Supercross events, promoters found that crowds often reacted the wildest when the winner performed a trick at the finish line.

At the same time, a huge trend of video documentation of professional riders practicing, jumping, and doing tricks emerged. The videos closely resembled skate

and snowboard videos, and following the 1993 release of *Crusty Demons of Dirt*, the sport of freestyle motocross took off with immense popularity. With the videos selling thousands of copies, many of the professionals were making money by racing and by jumping in the videos, which led to a rapid expansion of the sport.

One of the biggest boosts to the sport of freestyle was when Supercross champion Jeremy McGrath took finish-line victory jumps to a new level. Using his BMX roots, McGrath brought a new style of jumping to the stadium. He replaced the standard one-handed wave to the crowd with his signature move called the Nac-Nac. This jump consisted of whipping the bike sideways in the air and at the same time throwing a leg over the seat and extending it behind him, while looking back at the crowd. This move popularized the growing sport of freestyle motocross, and brought it to capacity-filled stadiums across the world. Soon even the people who had not seen or been involved in the video trend saw this new form of riding, and without a doubt it sparked a new flame in the already popular sport.

Another pioneer, 1998 Freestyle Motocross Champion and 1999 Vans Triple Crown winner Mike Metzger, has also been a constant innovator. Metzger was one of the original jumpers in *Crusty Demons of Dirt,* and he shocked the sport following the release of the video with freestyle moves such as the Heel Clicker, where the rider takes both feet from the pegs, brings them up and over the handlebars, and "clicks" them together in front of his number plate. Moves like this really set Metzger apart from other riders in the videos, and he continues to come up with and perfect similar tricks that were once inconceivable to people in the motorcycle industry.

Fox's *Terrafirma* is heralded as one of the sport's best videos and acted as a catalyst for the freestyle movement. Steve Lamson (pictured here) starred in the video alongside teammate Jeremy McGrath.

Jimmy Button handled a lot of the helmet cam work in *Steel Roots*, a freestyle film produced by Jeremy McGrath and Lawrence Lewis. Technology in filming has been a big part of the success encountered by the freeriding revolution.

In 1997, following countless new freestyle video releases, the sport really began to take off. As freestyle began to catch the eye of corporate and industry sponsors, money started flowing into the sport. Seeing the potential of other extreme sports and the popularity of this new hybrid form of motocross, a company named 4 Leaf Entertainment threw the first United States Freestyle Motocross event, which went over well. With the success of the event, 4 Leaf expanded to form the International Freestyle Motocross Association (IFMA) in 1998.

The formation of IFMA introduced a new level of freestyle motocross—jump contests. What was formerly a sideshow during the intermissions of overseas Supercross races and Arenacrosses was now an organized event by itself. The Free Air Festival Freestyle Motocross Tour began in 1998 and consisted of four stops: two in Las Vegas, one in Tacoma, Washington, and one in Lake Havasu, Arizona. Attracting big sponsors like Vans, the riders chased $175,000 in purse money throughout the tour.

Since that first year of organized competition, the sport has truly taken off. In 1999, freestyle motocross was seen at an unprecedented number of events, including premier extreme sports venues like ESPN's X-Games and even network giant NBC's Gravity Games. New promoters have also entered the game, and with companies like LXD and Supercross promoter PACE Motorsports now holding events in stadiums, freestyle motocross has broken out of its "sideshow" shell and is now considered a prime event.

The format for most freestyle contests starts with a number of entrants who compete in several heats; the top scorers move on to qualify for the main event where the big money is made. Each heat has a time limit of up to two minutes, and the riders do a variety of tricks over the different jumps. There are generally between three and five judges appointed to score the heats and final round. These judges determine final scores by combining points from five categories. These categories include Amplitude, Transitions, Degree of Difficulty, Originality, and Overall Impression.

Courses for the freestyle events often consist of a combination of wooden ramps and dirt jumps with gaps that range from about 60 to 90 feet in length. These big jumps help ensure that riders have enough airtime to perform all their tricks.

No other motorsport on the planet has taken off with the excitement that freestyle motocross has. Although no one can predict the future, it seems that freestyle motocross will definitely have a bright one. In the two years that it has existed, the sport has caught the full attention of the mainstream media. In the coming years, it will only grow. With the adrenaline-seeking trend of modern sports fans, freestyle motocross will undoubtedly hold a spot as one of the premier two-wheeled motorsport events.

With the evolution of a specialized sport such as freestyle motocross comes a similar evolution of specialized motorcycles and accessories designed to enhance performance. Although the bikes are basically the same as those used for motocross racing, there are some significant differences.

Before the discussion of parts and accessories, we must first mention motorcycle selection. Riders can choose from a wide variety of motorcycles when it comes to jumping, but the most common choice for most freestylers is a 250-cc, two-stroke machine. This is because 250s combine adequate horsepower with a lightweight maneuverability that makes them easy to throw around in the air.

Some riders prefer 125s because they are even lighter and more maneuverable than 250s, but most riders feel uncomfortable with the amount of power they have for clearing big gaps. Others prefer the controllable power of bikes like the Yamaha YZ 426F, which has a four-stroke engine that provides a smooth

Bad boy Brian Deegan was one of the first to take modifications seriously. Cutting away the side panels and the seat foam of his Honda CR250 gives him several places to grab while performing such rude aerial tricks as the Mulisha Grab and the Hart Attack.

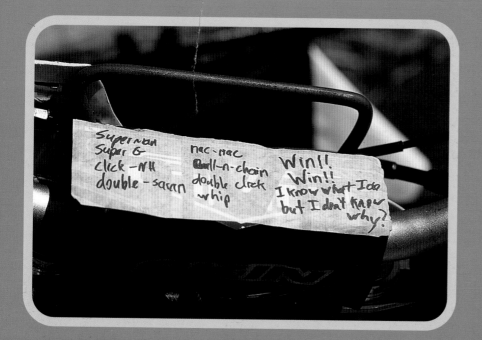

Justin Homan built this handmade grab handle so that he has a place to grab when doing Rodeos. Answer Pro Taper handlebars allow him better maneuverability on the front part of the bike, and the protective bar clamp cover makes a great place for him to mount his routine.

Homan also made this rear grab handle that attaches to the subframe. This is intended to make freestyle safer since he has a much easier time grabbing this handle than Brian Deegan has with his seat- and side panel–cutting method, which is another alternative.

delivery. Smooth delivery is beneficial on slippery surfaces like the wooden ramps often used in competitions and exhibitions.

Once a bike has been selected, the next step is to perform some modifications, which can range from small and inconspicuous to completely radical. Many of the changes that take place on freestyle bikes are "homemade" and done in someone's garage, a combination of ingenuity and necessity that has evolved based on the needs of specific tricks.

Modifications that can be purchased and professionally executed include many of the same things that are offered to beef up motocross racing bikes. Included in this list of mods are engine and suspension hop-ups offered by aftermarket companies like Pro Circuit and FMF. Of these modifications, the most important for freestylers is suspension work.

Stock suspension is much too soft for the 90-foot jumps that are common in the sport, and can be very dangerous during landings as well as takeoffs. The softness leads to bottoming, which can throw riders off and lead to a loss of balance in the air. To control this problem, stiffer springs are installed both in the forks and the shocks. Revalving is also performed to further reduce bottoming problems.

Engine enhancements aren't as necessary as suspension enhancements, but they are still pretty common. A variety of

These custom-built tall footpegs make it easier for Brian Deegan to get his feet over the seat when performing foot tricks. It may be only a slight variance, but every little inch counts when a rider is jumping at world-class level.

A Scott's Steering Stabilizer allows Deegan more control of the front end when executing No-Hander-Landers. Like a magician, it doesn't matter how hard the trick really is, as long as the crowd thinks it's life-threatening.

Trevor Vines studies his rendition of the track prior to his first practice session at the inaugural Gravity Games in Rhode Island. Although there are many things to prepare on a bike, there's also a lot that goes on behind the scenes before the engine is ever lit.

modifications can take place here. The most popular are pipe replacement and cylinder porting, both of which change the powerband and delivery.

One of the most common things riders do to customize their machines is seat foam cutting, which involves removing the seat from the bike, taking off the seat cover, and shaving down the foam. After the seat is reinstalled on the bike and the seat cover is replaced, the height of the seat is substantially lower. This is helpful when doing tricks like Can-Cans, Double Can-Cans, and Pendulums, all of which require riders to raise their legs up and over the saddle. With the seat even an inch lower than stock, it is much easier for riders to clear it with their

boots without getting hung up and crashing.

Some competitors also install taller footpegs. The combination of the shaved seat foam and the taller pegs creates a much smaller space that must be cleared for riders to make it over the seat with their feet. Travis Pastrana has taken this concept to an even further extreme, installing a "dry brake"—style gas tank that is commonly used by off-road riders for quick tank fills. For Pastrana, though, it does a different job. The dry brake gas system eliminates the bulky gas cap found on a stock bike. This means that Travis has one less thing to worry about catching his feet on.

Another trick that freestylers have borrowed from off-road riders is the use of

Travis Pastrana borrowed this dry brake from off-road racing. This shaves 2 full inches off the fuel tank height and makes it possible for him to do better foot tricks with less fear of getting his long legs tangled. Remember, the boy is over 6 feet tall, and there's not a lot of room for maneuvering on his RM 125!

Brian Deegan tapes up his controls to lessen the chance of getting a boot buckle or something else caught on a sharp edge. Deegan's rebel-like appearance may not show it, but he's actually one of the smartest riders competing.

steering stabilizers. Landings become much more stable and safe with these, and they are especially helpful for No-Hander-Landers. Without a steering stabilizer, the front end can get out of control much easier even if the rider lands just slightly sideways.

Another popular alteration you'll see in the pits at a freestyle event is the side panel cutout. This customization involves taking off the side number plates and cutting holes in them with a saw. These holes expose the frame, allowing riders to grab the subframe on tricks like the Superman Seat Grab.

A modification similar to the side panel cutout is the custom "grab handle" found on the machines of riders like Clifford Adoptante and Justin Homan. Grab handles are metal fabrications that attach to the subframe, where the rear seat bolts are located. Extending an inch or two above the seat, the grab handle is used in the same way as a side panel cutout, assisting with Superman Seat Grabs and Indian Airs, where riders extend their legs behind the motorcycle.

Grab handles are also found on the front of bikes, attached to the top triple clamp. Front grab handles are helpful for tricks like Rodeos, where riders need something to grab onto in front of the bike while in the air.

The revisions and alterations found on freestyle bikes are as unique as they are important. The right bike setup is crucial to freestyle jumping, and can often make the difference between pulling off a new trick and hitting the ground. Aftermarket items like stiffer suspension springs and engine hop-ups like pipes and porting are critical to proper performance, and make big jumps safer for the rider. The customization of motorcycles is equally important and represents the constant ingenuity of the competitors.

Mike Metzger

When people think of freestyle motocross, the first image that comes to mind is none other than Mike Metzger. The 23-year-old Quail Valley, California, resident is the undisputed pioneer of the sport, introducing motocross fans to an entirely new hybrid sport that was an immediate success. Freestyle motocross caught fire not only in the United States, but across the world, with jump contests in cities ranging from Sydney, Australia, to Paris, France.

With an amazing appearance in the video that started it all, Metzger had eager fans young and old alike lining up in droves to pick up a copy of *Crusty Demons of Dirt* in 1993. At the tender age of 17, Metzger was going bigger than anyone in the video, pulling moves like Heel Clickers that at the time were virtually unheard of. Although Metzger was also a competitive professional racer, he achieved unbelievable popularity and fame following the release of *Crusty Demons of Dirt*. Before long, Metzger was featured in video after video, establishing a loyal following of fans who were shelling out big bucks to see what kind of crazy jumps he would perform in order to outdo his previous video releases.

Metzger took his first ride on a motorcycle with his dad before he was even able to walk, and by the age of three he had his very own JR50, which he regularly practiced on until his first race at age six. Metzger was raised in a competitive family and was strongly encouraged to race by his father, a Southern California pro motocrosser.

Success on the track came fairly quickly to Metzger, and before long he was racking up championships and sponsors, including factory support from Suzuki. Although racing was going great for Metzger and he was developing a successful career, success came at a high cost in the form of injuries. When asked how many broken bones he has suffered, Metzger responded, "Too many—I don't even know the exact number anymore. I stopped counting a while ago, but I know it's over 20 now."

Between injuries, however, Metzger trains and rides hard. All of the training for motocross is what eventually developed his freestyle talents. Elaborating on the freestyle aspect of the sport, Metzger said, "Freestyle, to me, is just practice for racing."

Whatever he calls it, it is definitely a lucrative industry for him. Metzger is the 1998 IFMA Free Air Festival World Freestyle Motocross Champion, taking the first title of the relatively new but flourishing freeride organization.

Not only has Metzger been dominating the jump contests, but his video career has also continued to thrive. He has now starred in countless freestyle videos, and still loves doing it. Metzger feels that the videos have been great for the sport. At the same time, though, he believes that they are on the verge of over-exploitation, with people producing videos strictly for money rather than the love of the sport.

Metzger wants to keep racing motocross and competing in jump contests as long as his body can withstand the abuse. At that point, he is entertaining the ideas of street bike and Indy car racing. But whatever he does, you can be sure of two things—it will be some form of competitive racing, and no matter which one it is, Metzger will be dominating.

Ronnie Faisst

To Ronnie Faisst, freestyle motocross is nothing short of a miracle. His life has been turned upside down by the sport, all from a risky, last-minute decision he made a few years ago with his friend Brian Deegan.

The 22-year-old from Summer's Point, New Jersey, was in the middle of a struggling professional motocross career when an intervention of chance occurred in his life. While staying at Faisst's house in between the Budd's Creek and Southwick Nationals, Deegan recruited Faisst to film for a *Moto XXX video*, and Faisst had a blast. After the filming, Faisst was so excited about being in a video that he got caught up in the moment, dropped everything, and decided to go back to California with Deegan and become a video star.

Within the span of a few weeks, Faisst's dreams were already coming true, and between video shoots he was scheduled to ride on the Warp Tour, where he toured the country with several other athletes doing exhibitions. His life and career haven't slowed down a bit ever since.

main one being the fairness of the sport. Unlike the elite freestylers, the top factory motocrossers have a huge advantage over their competition because of the bikes they ride and the works parts they receive. In freestyle, bike selection and performance aren't as critically linked, making the competition more equal and allowing the best person to win. The costs of competition are also much lower with freestyle, and because there aren't as many competitors the riders make a better living.

Faisst plans to continue competing in freestyle events for at least 10 more years, and future plans include forming a new exhibition team called "The Flying Diablos." The Diablos will consist of a five-man team, including Faisst, Brian Deegan, Mike Cinqmars, Carey Hart, and Larry Linkogle, and will travel to select events with their own jump setups and ramps to do freestyle shows.

Faisst now lives in Corona, California, and along with friends Deegan and Linkogle leases a freestyle park in Lake Elsinore where he is able to practice his moves in between contests. Faisst is a consistent top-five finisher who has developed a style all his own. His extension of the tricks and the flexibility he incorporates into the execution of his moves are what characterize his unique style. Faisst credits the extension and flexibility of his body to his love of martial arts, which he has been involved in since age five.

Another cross-training activity that Faisst puts to use on his motorcycle is BMX jumping; he tries to ride his bicycle a few times a week. Besides keeping him from burning out, BMX is a great way to stay in shape for the quick freestyle runs he does in competitions, which are usually under two minutes. Faisst likes the short, intense format that freestyle uses much better than the 40-minute motos of outdoor racing, which are tough to train for.

According to Faisst, freestyle has several distinct advantages over motocross racing, the

Kris Rourke

Former motocross racer Kris Rourke had an interesting beginning to his freestyle career. The 20-year-old from Idaho was at an SMP freeride show near his hometown in 1998 when he got the wild idea to approach freestyle icon Mickey Dymond, who was attending the exhibition. Rourke asked Dymond if he would allow him to hit a few jumps, and after Dymond got the request cleared by the powers that be, Rourke was out there riding with his idols. When no one had the guts to be the first one to hit a 100-foot double, Rourke stepped up and cleared it. Immediately after landing, the freeride guys he looked up to were coming up to him, asking him what gear to hit the double in!

Needless to say, SMP allowed him to ride the rest of the show that night, and eventually offered him a sponsorship. In the span of less than a year, the ex-professional motocross racer was living out his dreams in the land of sun and surf, Southern California. He quit racing and turned into a full-time freerider, competing in contests almost weekly and making a good living at the same time.

Rourke got his start riding motorcycles after spending a few years at the BMX track, where he planted his jumping roots. When he was nine years old, his dad, who worked at a local motorcycle shop, could tell that Kris had an intense love for two wheels, and so he bought his son a dirt bike. With his BMX experience, it didn't take Rourke long to learn how to ride, and before he knew it, he was competing in local races. Within the time span of a couple of years, Rourke was competing in the pro class, where he won the Idaho State Championships three years in a row, along with an Arenacross in Salt Lake City, Utah.

Although he still loves racing, he prefers the jumping scene to the moto scene for one major reason: the training schedule. When he was racing Nationals, he was forced to train daily, almost nonstop. His body was starting to feel the effects of the constant abuse, and with 15 broken bones by the time he was 17, Rourke saw an opportunity to take on an entirely new sport that didn't have him diving into the first turn with 20 other hungry racers.

His choice has been a good one thus far, as the only injury he has experienced freestyling is a torn anterior cruciate ligament in his knee. Rourke feels that he will be able to continue his freestyle career for several more years, and barring any major disasters, he plans on competing in events until he is at least 35 years old.

Rourke has some pretty big plans for his future, and is currently working on some top-secret new moves for the upcoming season. If his new tricks resemble the ones that he is pulling now, the competition better watch out, as Rourke is known for his huge tricks and smooth jumping style.

Brian Deegan

Successful motorcycle riding is not a new concept to 24-year-old Brian Deegan. The Canyon Lake, California, resident has carried

this theme throughout his career, both in motocross and Supercross, as well as in freestyle riding. In fact, Deegan is by far the most successful freestyle competitor out there, with a racing resume as impressive as the Indian Air Superman Seat Grabs that he throws.

Deegan began his motorcycle career at age 8, and was racing by 10. Within the span of a few short years, Brian was already racking up championships, with a multitude of wins at suchmajor NMA race events as Ponca City. By 18, Deegan was ready to go pro, and made the step in 1992. Working his way up to the top, Deegan started to be a major threat both indoors and out, and in 1997 he accomplished the biggest dream of any aspiring young racer—he won a Supercross main event. With that huge victory came plenty of controversy, though, which was only a foreshadowing of what was to come in Deegan's career.

After his win at the first round of the 1997 Supercross series in Los Angeles, Deegan was so excited that he decided to "ghost ride" his bike over the finish line to celebrate the win, causing not only the fans to scream, but the AMA as well. They labeled the stunt "dangerous" and fined Deegan $1,000. The fine and lectures didn't discourage Deegan, however; he continued to score several top-five finishes in the outdoor Nationals later in the year.

Around this time, Deegan began starring in some of the big freestyle motocross videos that were taking the MX community by storm. Soon he became known as one of the top freestyle athletes, and when contests were formed, Deegan competed in them and established himself as a top name in freestyle.

With all of the money being pumped into the sport, Deegan soon discovered that he could make more money by doing what he really loved—going out and having fun with his friends, freeriding on his motorcycle—than he could by racing.

Once his freestyle career began to flourish, Deegan combined his popularity with that of his friend Larry Linkogle's, and the two of them joined together to form the Metal Mulisha. The Mulisha began with the two riders just messing around, writing on their bikes with Magic Markers. From there, the two decided to have some stickers made, and T-shirts and hats followed. Fans took an immediate liking to the name as well

as the image, making the company so successful that Linkogle and Deegan are barely able to keep up with the constant demand for clothes.

Balancing the Metal Mulisha clothes line with his busy freestyle competition schedule is no easy task for Deegan, but he seems to be doing a pretty good job with both sides of his career. He recently captured the LXD Freestyle World Championship, and before that he proved himself a top rider by earning a second at NBC's Gravity Games and a third at the ESPN X-Games in 1999.

Deegan plans on competing for at least five more years, at which time he hopes to have enough money invested to retire and run the Metal Mulisha full time. For now, though, he will continue racking up wins and stirring up controversy on the freestyle circuit. Although the press seems to consistently label him a "rebel" and expose his dark side, in reality Brian Deegan is a quiet guy who honestly likes to help people out. Deegan gained his bad boy reputation simply because of his opposition to the corporate butt-kissing of motocross racing, which he cites as his main reason for quitting the professional racing circuit. The black outfit and the spiked shoulder pads are just his way of expressing himself as an individual. Whatever your personal take on him, though, it is impossible to argue the fact that Deegan is one of the most talented, hardest-working riders out there.

Larry Linkogle

Offending people is nothing new to freestyle rider Larry Linkogle. Going against the grain is the motivating force behind the 22-year-old's assault on the motorcycle industry, and he has slowly gained a reputation as freestyle's bad boy. He, along with fellow Metal Mulisha teammate Brian Deegan, has exposed a dark side to the sport that upsets some and electrifies others.

The Temecula, California, resident has been riding for more than 11 years, starting on 80-cc machines and working his way up through local motocross races to become a pro at age 15. A natural on motorcycles, Link began his racing career only two months after he first started riding. His love for racing turned sour after a few years, however, and he began to feel that there were too many politics involved for professional riders. A few

short years into his racing career, he was burnt out and not having fun anymore. His passion for practicing and jumping with his friends surpassed his racing desire, and it wasn't long before racing was completely sidelined.

Following a move to Temecula where his parents bought a house in the country, Linkogle found himself with tons of land. With the help of Mulisha teammate Deegan he built the first "freestyle park." The Mulisha Compound consisted of huge jumps that were only open to a select few for riding, and established motocross stars like Jeremy McGrath were strictly prohibited from riding there. It became a breeding ground for freestyle innovations as well as a popular spot for video production, and the Compound was soon featured in countless videos that shaped the freestyle revolution.

Besides riding for sheer enjoyment, Linkogle also credits his love for the motorcycle with its ability to let out pent-up aggressions. Link is very hostile toward the world, and he vents this hostility when he hits 90-foot jumps. When not on his motorcycle, Linkogle plays the bass guitar in a death-metal band, which is another way for him to release built-up aggression.

Linkogle has been competing in freestyle motocross since the beginning. This involvement has made him a witness to the sport's rapid growth, which he detests. Link feels that there has been a great exploitation of freestyle motocross and claims that companies that once thought of freestyle as an embarrassment to motocross are now trying to capitalize on its popularity. Because of this, Linkogle rarely competes anymore, and will only ride at events promoted by certain companies. This hasn't dampened Linkogle's love of the sport one bit, though, and he still rides for the same reason he did from day one—the love of riding motorcycles.

CLIFFHANGER

The **Cliffhanger** is one of several tricks brought to the sport by freestyle phenomenon Travis Pastrana. Although it didn't take long for others to follow Pastrana's footsteps and perform the maneuver, Travis was credited with inventing the move.

Before long, magazine and video audiences worldwide were seeing the move performed by Pastrana at several locations, the most notable being the popular filming location of Beaumont, California.

The Cliffhanger consists of the rider almost completely leaving the bike, holding on to the machine in the air by only his feet, which are placed under the handlebars, and raising his hands straight up toward the sky. The higher the hands are raised and the farther the body is extended, the more stylish the trick is, and the better score it receives by judges during jump contests.

On the following pages, Mike Metzger illustrates the Cliffhanger, showing us the full extension of the trick.

Mike Metzger
Lake Elsinore, California

CLIFFHANGER

Mike Metzger explains the
CLIFFHANGER

"The **Cliffhanger** is a fairly tough move that Pastrana invented a few years ago. It's a little sketchier than others because your hands leave the grips for so long, and you are holding on to your bike in midair with only your feet. In this first photo, I'm coming off of the lip, with my back wheel a foot or two in the air. I have already begun to throw my legs off of the pegs and up towards the front of the bike. I am keeping my shoulders nice and centered over the handlebars to keep me stable in the air."

"In this second shot, I'm just getting ready to grip beneath my handlebars, at the top of my fork tubes, with my feet. I start to squeeze my inside thigh muscles and calves in order to hold myself tight to the bike. Once I fully grip my fork tubes with my legs, I am at the point where I make sure everything is level, and I'm ready to take my hands off."

"With my hands off of the handlebars, I'm extending my shoulders and back. I am also starting to straighten my torso, bringing it back towards the rear fender. I am beginning to throw my arms back, the whole time keeping my inner thighs squeezed tight, as this is now my only way of holding on to the bike."

"In this fourth picture, my body is just about at full extension. You'll notice that I have thrown back my hands in the 'suicide' position, which is obviously just an optional style thing that I sometimes add to the trick. I always try to keep my legs nice and straight, because the farther they are extended, the better looking the trick will be."

"Here I am starting to return my hands from the suicide position behind my back, towards the front of the bike. My altitude is starting to drop, so I am also beginning to bring my butt down a little more towards the seat, but not too far yet. I have also spotted my landing, which is important by this point."

"In this sixth shot, I have started to reach for my handlebars, and am just about to make contact with the grips. It is important that I continue squeezing my legs on the fork tubes, and make sure that I don't start to lower them yet. I want to have a good grip on the bars before I move my legs."

"By this time, I have reassured myself that I have a good grip on the handlebars, and once I am sure of that, I start to bring my legs down from their position under the bars, towards the footpegs."

"In this final shot, I've got both my hands on the grips and my feet just about on the pegs. You can see that I am looking ahead at where I am going to land, and I am now confident that I will have a smooth landing. The only thing in my head by now is the plans that I have for jumping the next hit!"

BAR HOP

The **Bar Hop** does not have an officially recognized inventor, but most of the sources interviewed for this book claim that 6-foot, 4-inch freestyle giant Shawn Highland should be credited with the honors. Highland was seen doing the trick while filming the original *Moto XXX* video back in 1997 on a huge step-up.

Although Bar Hops might not look as radical as some of the other tricks the pros do, looks are deceiving with this maneuver. A rider performs the trick by raising both feet up and over the handlebars, sticking them straight out over the front fender, and bringing them back over the bars before returning them to the pegs. The reason for the increased difficulty of the Bar Hop is the chance a rider could catch a foot on the bars, causing a crash.

Riders best known for extending this trick the farthest are Jeremy "Twitch" Stenberg, Ronnie Faisst, and Clifford Adoptante, all of whom frequently perform Bar Hops during their freestyle contest runs. Adoptante has extended the trick one step farther by inventing the Sterilizer, a variation of the Bar Hop where the trick is performed normally, but instead of bringing his legs back over the bars and landing, Adoptante lands the Bar Hop with his legs out in front of the bars and fender while sitting his butt on the crossbar pad.

Reagan Sieg
Murrieta, California

BAR HOP

Ronnie Faisst explains the
BAR HOP

1 "The Bar Hop is a pretty gnarly trick. Even though I'm over the top of the bike and I can pretty much see what's going on, it's still one of the toughest tricks because it's hard to get both feet up, over, and through the handlebars. I approached this jump in third gear, with my body in a neutral, 'attack' position and my head looking forward."

2 "Almost immediately after I launch off of the lip, about 3 or 4 feet into the air, I bring my knees up to my chest as far as absolutely possible. I have to almost exaggerate the movement to make sure that I clear the bars. I sometimes bring my knees up so far that I actually hit my helmet with my knee guards."

"At midflight extension, I do a double front kick through my handlebars. This trick requires a lot of flexibility, and to make it look its best, a rider should try to kick his legs out as straight as possible. Also, riders need to make sure that they're holding on tight to the grips in the air."

"After I'm past the midway point in my flight, I begin to bring the trick down by pulling in my knees towards my chest again. I keep my head very high to allow even more clearance for my legs, and I make sure that they're bent enough before I try to clear the bars."

"Now that I know my knees are bent far enough, I start to pull them down over the handlebars. This is probably the most nerve-wracking moment of the trick. As you can see from the photo, I have my knees bent as far as they will go, and I'm still only clearing the top of my Pro Tapers by an inch or two."

BAR HOP

"Once I know that my boots have made it completely over the bars, the trick is pretty much downhill from there. All I have to remember to do now is separate my feet to get them over the gas tank and seat, and begin to lower them toward the pegs."

"At this point, I've separated my boots and legs, and I have just about brought them down far enough to touch the pegs. Even before they make contact, though, I am already gripping the sides of the bike's frame with the inside of my legs. This helps me brace for the landing, and also keeps the bike stable."

The **Heel Clicker** is one of the original moves that really blew up the sport of freestyle motocross. Credited with the invention of this move is the tall, lanky, ex-motocross racer Gordon Ward, who was performing Heel Clickers way back in the 1980s while celebrating race wins.

To perform this trick, which is now considered one of the easier tricks of freestyle motocross, the rider lifts both legs up and over the handlebars; then, with his hands still on the handlebars, he wraps his legs around his elbows and touches his boots together in front of the front number plate.

Many of the contributors to this book recommend that this be the first freestyle trick beginning riders try, as the freestyler does not have to commit to the trick like they would with other, more difficult moves. Riders can begin learning the Heel Clicker by simply starting with a No-Footer, and bringing it up a little higher with each try until it feels comfortable for them to swing their legs all the way in front of the number plate.

In the subsequent sequence, Kris Rourke shows us how to perform the Heel Clicker at his practice jump in Murrieta, California.

Trevor Vines
Providence, Rhode Island

HEEL CLICKER

Kris Rourke explains the
HEEL CLICKER

"Coming up to the approach of this steep double jump, the first thing that I am thinking about is making sure that I have enough speed to clear the gap without having to make any additional changes or compensations in the air. I have to make sure that my timing is on perfectly, while at the same time trying to get my body weight forward towards the front of the bike. Everything must be positioned perfectly so that when the bike comes off the lip, it settles well in the air, in a balanced position. When doing a Heel Clicker, the bike needs to be level in the air."

"In this picture, I'm basically just waiting for the bike to level out in the air. With Heel Clickers, I don't have to worry about throwing the trick right away, I can relax for a little while before raising my legs. By this time, I double-check the lift I have gotten off the first jump, making sure I will clear the jump right. I try to spot my landing as soon as possible so I feel comfortable in the air."

"For this shot, I am starting to bring my body weight back towards the rear of the bike a little more, while at the same time beginning to raise my legs up and off of the footpegs. When doing Heel Clickers, my butt will eventually raise up to the point of being almost on top of the handlebars, but before I get in this position I must first bring my weight back, almost to the rear fender."

"When my legs start to make their way up and over the ends of the handlebars, at the same time I have to bring my body up more towards the tank and the bars. My legs are a little bit above the bars now, and I have made sure that I brought my legs out far enough away to clear them and not get hung up. I can now make little adjustments in the air to the balance of the bike by pulling up on either side of the bars accordingly."

HEEL CLICKER

5

"In this photo, my feet are coming up to the point where they are starting to 'click.' Some riders, when clicking their feet, have trouble going from the fourth frame here to the fifth frame. The trick is that the rider has to bend his knees a lot to force them to go all of the way around his arms. Some riders, especially those with short legs, actually have to pull their elbows in so they can click their feet. As long as a rider can get his legs up high enough to touch his elbows he should be fine. It just takes a little time to get to this point."

6

"Here, I have already clicked my heels together, and I am starting to bring my legs back down around my bars. A helpful hint on this step is to use the momentum of clicking them together to help bring them around far enough to clear the grips. There is also the option here of going back and doing a second click once a rider gets a bit more advanced. On this one, though, I am just coming down normally."

"Now that I have brought my legs down past my grips, I start to think about the landing. Before, when my boots were up in front of my body, I lost my bearings. Here, my legs are farther down, so I can again see in front of my bike and spot my landing again. I begin adjusting my body, and the main concentration now is to get my legs down safely."

"I am starting to set up even more for the landing now, trying to get my body weight a little farther back towards the rear of the bike. I want the front wheel to land first because of the steepness of the landing jump, so the bike needs to drop a little up there. Here, I still have time to make little adjustments to the bike, like hitting my rear brake to drop the front end or gassing it to keep the bike from doing an endo."

"I now know exactly where I am going and where I will touch down. Like I said earlier, this jump has a very steep down slope, so I am bringing the front end down more to make a nice, smooth landing. I am set up well, and you can see that my head and my arms are both raised, ready to soak up the hit of the landing."

HART ATTACK

Of the many freestyle tricks that professional jumpers are currently pulling at events, not many receive more applause than the Hart Attack. As the name suggests, Carey Hart started the craze, and it didn't take long for others to try to follow in his footsteps. The trick is so difficult, though, that at the time of publication there were only two riders doing justice to it: Hart himself, of course, and Brian Deegan.

The **Hart Attack** is one of several tricks based on the Superman Seat Grab, which Hart also brought to the sport. The setups of the two tricks are very similar, but the main difference is that with the Hart Attack, the rider extends himself vertically behind the bike, whereas in the Superman Seat Grab the legs are brought out horizontally, in line with the ground. The closer to straight up and down the rider is when he is behind the rear fender, the more impressive the trick is.

Because the Hart Attack is so difficult, riders must approach this trick with extreme caution. Riders learn the trick by first making sure they can do regular Superman Seat Grabs, and after they are throwing them effortlessly, they start to extend them a little farther each time until they are finally throwing their legs and body up vertically.

Metal Mulisha founder and team rider Brian Deegan demonstrates the Hart Attack in the following sequence.

Carey Hart
Arrowhead Pond

Brian Deegan explains the
HART ATTACK

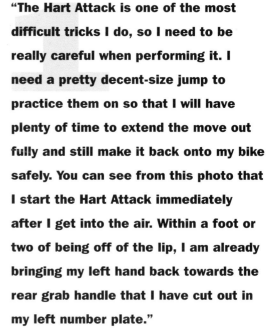

"The Hart Attack is one of the most difficult tricks I do, so I need to be really careful when performing it. I need a pretty decent-size jump to practice them on so that I will have plenty of time to extend the move out fully and still make it back onto my bike safely. You can see from this photo that I start the Hart Attack immediately after I get into the air. Within a foot or two of being off of the lip, I am already bringing my left hand back towards the rear grab handle that I have cut out in my left number plate."

"In this second photo, my hand has made contact with the grab handle, which is an important first step. The next part of the trick is to begin to bring my legs back to the rear end of the bike. My left leg naturally goes back a little before my right leg because of the fact that I am grabbing with my left side, but this is OK. You can still see that my right leg is coming off of the footpeg, and I have plenty of time to get it back to the rear of the bike."

HART ATTACK

"By now, both feet are up off of the pegs and making their way back to the rear end, and up to this point the trick still looks like a Superman Seat Grab. I have a firm grip on the motorcycle with both hands, my right hand on the grip and my left hand on the grab handle. The main thing that I am concentrating on at this point is bringing my legs back, and I also double check the balance of the bike. I want to make sure that the bike is stable in the air before I go upside down."

"Here I am continuing the extension, and my legs are making their way up towards the sky. I have already gone past the point of a standard Superman Seat Grab. One thing I need to double check here is that the bike is stable up to this point. I don't want to be front-end high, or low for that matter, because once I extend my legs way up, there is not much I can do to make corrections."

"In this fifth photo, I am nearing full extension of the Hart Attack. The bike is still nice and stable, with the front end just slightly higher than the rear. This is the position that the motorcycle needs to be in. Even though my legs and body are almost upside down by now, notice that my head is still looking forward and almost level. This is important, as I do not want to look straight down to my seat, or I will become disoriented."

"In this frame, I am coming down from full extension. To do this, I can't just rely on gravity to pull me down. I have to pull myself down with both hands. You will notice that my handlebars are turning to the right, and there is a reason for this. It is because I am pulling down with my right hand. This is alright; it can be fixed later."

"I am still coming down from the Hart Attack, and my handlebars and front end are continuing to turn. There is plenty of time and height left, but I want to get back to a normal position on the bike as soon as possible. I will keep my hand on the grab handle a little longer, until my legs get down farther towards the footpegs."

"In this final photo, I have released my left hand from the side grab handle and brought it up to the grip. This will help straighten out the bars before touching down, as you can see from the photo. My legs are inches from the pegs, and I only have about 5 feet until I land. Once I am back into a proper position on the bike, I will continue standing up to brace for the shock of landing."

DOUBLE CAN-CAN

The **Double Can-Can** is a trick that, like many other freestyle motocross moves, has evolved from tricks that have been around for quite some time. This particular move originated from the standard Can-Can, which has been around for years and involves the rider extending a single leg over the seat to the opposite side of the motorcycle. As with many other freestyle tricks, the Double Can-Can originated from BMX jumping.

Double Can-Cans differ from the standard Can-Can in that the rider brings both feet up and over the seat simultaneously, kicking them as straight out as possible before returning them back over the seat and to the footpegs. The farther out the legs are extended the better, and most riders try to rotate their bodies and heads over to the side, where they look at the crowd during competitions.

Many riders incorporate Double Can-Cans in their runs. Variations of the trick include landing "Annie Oakley" style (where riders land side-saddled in the Double Can-Can position with both legs over the seat), the Switchblade (which is an inverted version of the move), and the Pendulum (where riders swing their legs to both sides of the seat before landing).

Mike Metzger
San Diego, California

DOUBLE CAN-CAN

Larry Linkogle explains the
DOUBLE
CAN-CAN

"I like to find a big jump to do my Double Cans on so I can throw them out nice and fat, but they can be done on smaller jumps. This jump, at the Metal Mulisha compound in Lake Elsinore, California, is about 90 feet long, which is just about the perfect gap for the trick. I start the jump as I would start any jump, with plenty of speed and in a regular body position, standing up with my elbows and head up."

1

"About 5 feet off of the takeoff, I start to throw the trick. I still continue to have my body in an upright position on the bike, but now you can see that I have just started to pull up my legs in preparation to pull them up and over the seat. I am also gripping the bike with my knees slightly in order to get the maximum height out of the jump."

2

"Now I am probably about 10 feet off of the lip; I know that I must start acting quickly so that I will have enough time to pull the trick. I keep pulling my legs up, putting a special emphasis on bringing my right leg a little higher than my left because I have to clear the seat with it."

"With both feet up fairly high now, I start to concentrate on bringing my knees up towards my chest. This keeps them really high, which will allow for maximum extension later on in the trick. I start to turn my head towards the side of the bike that I will kick my legs out on, which will help me turn my body farther over during the peak moment of the trick."

"This photo shows the point where I am just about at full extension of the Double Can-Can. Both of my legs are well over the seat and to the side of the bike. You can also see that my head is turned to the side of extension, and so is my body, which followed my head. The back of my bike is also whipped just a small amount, which adds a bit more style to the trick."

"Now I am starting to bring the trick back down from the peak. The best way to do this is to turn my neck back towards the straight-ahead position, while at the same time bringing my legs closer to the top of the seat."

"I have brought my legs back over the seat now, and as you can see, I don't have to bring them into my chest as far as I do on the way out. I just need to make sure that I have cleared the seat with my boots so that they won't get caught up and cause me to crash."

"By now, I have regained control of the bike, and although I haven't actually made contact with my footpegs, it is only a matter of time until they naturally float back down. I have spotted my landing, and my body is in a position that I will be able to take the shock of the landing without a problem."

"Here, I am getting ready to touch down on the back side of the second jump. My boots have made their way down to the pegs, and I have plenty of time to regain complete control before landing. My knees and elbows are slightly bent to absorb the shock of the landing, and I am comfortable in my distance. I know that I will clear the jump, so from here I just sit back and wait to land."

PENDULUM

The **Pendulum** is very similar to the Double Can-Can and involves the same basic principles, but differs because after the rider has brought both legs over one side of the seat and extended them outwards, the trick isn't over yet—the rider must then bring both legs over the saddle again, extending them out on the other side. From here, the rider has the option of completing the trick by putting both feet back on the pegs, or extending them out once again, back to the other side of the bike where the trick began. This extra extension is obviously much harder and requires slightly more time in the air, so riders are awarded more points.

Pendulums are much easier for shorter riders who have smaller legs, which are easier to swing back and forth in the air. Because of this, smaller riders like Tommy Clowers are able to do this trick with much less effort than the taller guys. The trick also takes some very quick moving on the rider's part, so they need to make sure that they have mastered Double Can-Cans with plenty of time to spare before they even think about attempting moves like the Pendulum.

In the accompanying sequence, Mike Metzger shows us how he performs the trick using a 90-foot-long jump at the Metal Mulisha jump compound in Lake Elsinore, California.

PENDULUM

Tommy Clowers
Costa Mesa, California

Mike Metzger explains the PENDULUM

1 "The Pendulum is basically a spin-off of the Double Can-Can, but instead of going back down to the pegs after I throw my legs out, I swing them to the other side of the bike and do another Double Can. Because of this, I need a decent-size jump. This one is about 90 feet, which is adequate. In the first shot, I am thinking about hitting the lip perfectly straight, centered, and staying comfortable on the bike. I am also standing up and looking straight ahead, preparing to launch into the air."

2 "In the second picture, I'm getting more balanced on the bike, with my upper torso up near my handlebars. I am also getting ready to throw my legs up already, because I can't wait very long on Pendulums to bring my legs over the seat."

"By this point, I am already raising my legs pretty high, with my left leg nearing the top of my seat. I start to throw my legs out to the right side, because that is my goofy side. I always start on my non-favorite side first, to get it out of the way so I feel comfortable later on in the trick."

"In the fourth picture, I am getting ready to throw my feet around to the side of the bike, and bust out a big Double Can. I start to twist my hips first, and I also am thinking about making sure that I clear my seat completely with my boots."

"By the fifth shot, I am pretty much at the peak extension for the first Double Can-Can. Once I feel that I have reached the full extension, instead of hanging it out there like I would normally, I immediately start to rotate my hips back so that I can begin bringing my legs to the other side."

5

6 "Here I am centered over the bike, coming back over the seat. I have to really be careful not to catch my feet here. To prevent this, I almost exaggerate my knees going towards my chest, clearing my seat by a good few inches."

7 "Now I throw the trick to my left side, my preferred side, where I do another Double Can-Can. I still have plenty of time to bring the trick to this side because I have done everything so fast up to this point."

"I am hitting the peak extension on the left side of the Pendulum, throwing my legs out as far as possible. How far I bring them out really depends on how much time I have left before landing the trick and how fast I've moved up to this point."

"Here I'm getting ready to bring my body back to a normal riding position. I throw my right leg over the seat, making sure that I clear the seat and don't catch my boot. I am looking at the landing, making sure that I am going to touch down perfectly."

"In this final frame, I have both of my feet back to their regular position over the pegs. My head is forward and I'm balanced over the handlebars, with my shoulders and my elbows up, ready to land. If I have time, I even try to squeeze the bike a little with my boots to brace myself a little more for the landing."

NAC-NAC

The **Nac-Nac** has a very important history in the sport of freestyle motocross. Jeremy McGrath made this maneuver his signature victory celebration trick, and performed Nac-Nacs in stadiums across the world on the final laps of his winning races. What made this so important to freestyle motocross was that the move brought the underground sport to fans everywhere, increasing the interest in and acceptance of the sport.

Nac-Nacs are performed by a rider whipping his bike sideways, taking a leg off of the pegs, and extending it back behind the seat while at the same time turning his body over and looking at the crowd.

During the best Nac-Nacs, the rider extends a leg out and straightens it, with the bike completely sideways. Although the trick has been around for years, it is still quite difficult to do a really good, extended Nac-Nac, and when it is done right, it is quite impressive. Riders including Mike Metzger, Ronnie Faisst, and Carey Hart have taken the trick to a new level by inverting and whipping their bikes so far that they truly challenge the laws of gravity.

Showing us the proper technique of McGrath's Nac-Nac on the subsequent pages is freestyle rider Ronnie Faisst, who performs the trick at his practice track, the Metal Mulisha compound in Lake Elsinore, California.

NAC-NAC

Travis Pastrana

Providence, Rhode Island

Ronnie Faisst explains the
NAC-NAC

"Nac-Nacs are probably one of the coolest-feeling tricks that I have learned lately, and they really aren't that hard to do. They feel cool because I'm whipping out my bike, and at the same time taking my leg off. I approach this hit, which is about 70 feet long, in third gear about mid-throttle. I actually lean the bike over on the face of the jump like I'm going for a mellow whip."

"From here, you can see that I have set up for a whip, and am throwing the bike sideways. I haven't begun the Nac-Nac yet, because I am still gaining altitude and I need to get the bike a little more sideways."

"Now I've got the bike pretty sideways, so I will start to prepare for the trick. As you can see in the photo, my right leg has just begun to come off of the footpeg, and is about an inch above it."

"I am now fully committed to the Nac-Nac, and my right leg is kicking out behind me. If you look closely, you'll notice that my head and body are both turning to the right. This helps me get my leg over the seat and turn far enough over to make the trick look good."

5 "Here, I am at full extension of the trick. My head and body are still twisted way to the right, and this helps me tweak out the Nac-Nac to its fullest extent. Another hint to help extend Nac-Nacs even further is to concentrate on throwing a full back-kick off of the back of the bike, instead of just throwing it to the side."

6 "I'm coming down from the peak of the jump here, and need to start bringing the trick back. The easiest way for a rider to do this is for him to pretend that he is getting on the bike, on the ground, and swing his leg over the seat. I need to make sure that I get my boot well over the seat, because if I get my boot caught, I'm in trouble!"

"Again, I'm making sure that my boot is going to clear the saddle, and I swing my head and body all the way to the left. Remember, where your head goes, your body follows. I start to spot the landing, and get both feet on the pegs."

"By now, I've spotted my landing, and I'm coming down nose-first a little. This is natural because of the whip motion that happens when executing a Nac-Nac. I just need to make sure that I am standing up, and ready to brace myself for the landing."

SUPERMAN

The **Superman** follows the Nac-Nac in Supercross star Jeremy McGrath's list of contributions to the sport of freestyle motocross. McGrath borrowed this trick from BMX bicycle jumpers, who have been doing the maneuver for quite some time. The Superman was an immediate hit in the motocross world, and McGrath wowed Supercross fans both in the United States and overseas with the move.

Guys like Mike Metzger soon followed suit, and brought the Superman to a new level by extending the trick even further than McGrath could.

The Superman is performed by the rider taking both feet off of the pegs and extending them out behind the rear fender, causing separation between the rider and the bike. The rider, once extended from the bike, is connected by only the hands on the grips. The rider's body is parallel to the seat, and the straighter, stiffer, and farther away from the bike the rider is, the higher scoring the Superman will be.

Compared to the other tricks in this book, the Superman is considered an intermediate level move. It takes a considerable amount of upper body strength to pull off. Demonstrating the trick is Mike Metzger, a master at the Superman.

SUPERMAN

Mike Metzger
Lake Elsinore, California

Mike Metzger explains the
SUPERMAN

"I approach the takeoff of at least a 75- or 80-foot jump in third gear on a 250, and try to be in a standing-up and neutral body position. My suspension is compressed, and I make sure both ends remain as equal as possible off the lip to keep the bike stable."

"Throwing the Superman as soon as I can is important to allow enough time in the air. About 4 feet off the lip, I start the trick by pulling my feet off of the pegs first, and bringing the front end of the bike up slightly. My knees go up to my handlebar height almost immediately."

"Here I continue to bring my feet and legs up to gain more altitude for them, and I move my upper body far forward, keeping my head past the handlebars and towards the front fender to keep my weight in front. My elbows are also bent a little bit so that I don't drift back."

"Now that I am off of the bike completely, I am concentrating on putting as much space between me and my bike as possible. I haven't tried to straighten my legs out yet because I'm still gaining altitude and getting my body forward."

"At this point, I'm at the peak of my air time, and extending myself away from the bike. I try to bring my legs as far as I can from the seat and rear fender, because it looks way fatter when there is a big gap between my legs and the seat. I also keep a good grip on the handlebars, as I am now so far from the bike that if I let go of the grips, there is no chance of saving it."

"As I begin my descent downwards, I pull fairly hard on the bars to get myself back towards the center point of my bike. I keep my elbows up and bend them slightly, thinking the whole time about bringing my chest towards the crossbar pad. My knees are also naturally bending a lot as they make their way towards the pegs."

"A trick here to help ensure a smooth transition down to the bike is to pull my head back away from the front fender. This will bring my legs down towards the bike a little faster, allowing me to restore myself to a comfortable position."

"By now, I am able to spot my landing, so I know that I had better get back on the motorcycle and be ready to land. My feet go back to the pegs almost automatically, and my upper body has returned to an almost normal position. I definitely don't want to be way up towards the front anymore, or it's gonna hurt when I land!"

"By this point in the trick, I better be back to a normal position. Once my feet have found the pegs, I grab the sides of the bike hard with my legs and knees, and get ready to land. That's pretty much it, but remember, everyone does the trick a little different, and there are a few different variations. Riders should adapt their own style when doing Supermans, and shouldn't get hung up trying to do it the same way that someone else does."

SUPERMAN
SEAT GRAB

An extension of the Superman is a trick called the **Superman Seat Grab.** Even more impressive than the Superman itself, this trick was again brought over from the BMX world, though this time it wasn't from Supercross star Jeremy McGrath, but rather freestyle rider Carey Hart.

The trick's setup is similar to the Superman's, with the rider's feet extended outwards. During the Superman Seat Grab, however, the rider lets go of the left side of the bars and grabs either a cutout in the rear number plate or a grab handle that has been previously installed. With his body moved toward the back of the bike, the rider is able to extend the bike way out in front of himself, almost floating behind the machine.

There are many variations of the Superman Seat Grab. At the 1999 Gravity Games, Carey Hart and Brian Deegan were seen doing the trick by taking both hands off the handlebars, bringing them back even farther behind the bike. At the same event, Carey Hart also busted out the Hart Attack, which is basically a Superman Seat Grab. Instead of being horizontal from the bike, however, the rider extends his body to an almost vertical position, "handstand" style. The Indian Air also originated from the Superman Seat Grab, and here the rider does the original trick, but extends his legs out to do a scissors kick behind the bike before putting his feet back on the pegs.

Whichever way they are done, the Superman and its variations are some of the most impressive and difficult tricks out there. On the following pages, Metal Mulisha rider Larry Linkogle shows us his interpretation of the Superman Seat Grab on his practice track in Lake Elsinore, California.

Larry Linkogle
Lake Elsinore, California

Larry Linkogle explains the
SUPERMAN
SEAT GRAB

"Superman Seat Grabs are a lot of fun, but they're harder to do than the regular Supermans. A rider should make sure that he can do a Superman with little or no problem before he tries to pull a Superman Seat Grab. Although I've seen Deegan bust them on a 70 footer, I like to have a 90-foot jump to do them on so that I've got plenty of time to extend them. I hit the jump with enough speed so that I don't have to worry about clearing the gap, and I am standing nice and tall."

"About 5 feet in the air, after I've made sure that my bike is going the right way and is not too front-end high or going into an endo position, I start to reach back and feel for the grab handle that I have cut into the side of my number plate. My head is looking forward, and at the same time I reach for the handle I begin to take my feet off of the pegs."

"Here, I've found the grab handle, and I'm beginning to get high enough in the air that I feel comfortable to start the extension of my legs. I make sure that I'm holding the grab handle tightly, and when I throw my legs back, I do it as quickly as possible in one fast motion."

"A helpful hint to extend the trick is to throw the bike way out in front, using both arms. Continue holding on tightly to the grab handle, and use both arms to keep the bike nice and stable in the air. The front end needs to be slightly higher than the rear, but not too much."

5 "This is full extension, and once I'm in this position, I concentrate on holding it here as long as possible. Some riders keep their feet pretty close together here, but I prefer to separate them because it makes the trick look a lot better and more extended."

6 "After I've held the Seat Grab out for as long as I possibly can, I begin to get back on the bike. The easiest way to do this is to pull the whole machine back towards my body with both hands. This should all be done in the same motion, but my legs will naturally come back first."

7 "My feet continue their way towards the pegs, and I now feel confident in the fact that I will be able to make the landing with plenty of time, so I release the grab handle with my left hand and start to reach for the handlebars. I'm bringing my upper body forward in an effort to get my weight and inertia towards the front of the bike."

8 "With a couple of feet to spare before I touch down the wheels, I am completely back on my bike and ready for the landing. With jumps that are 90-foot-plus, I have to make sure I have enough time to gain complete control of the bike before I land so that I can absorb the shock."

SWITCHBLADE

The **Switchblade,** an advanced variation of the Double Can-Can, was introduced by Mike Metzger. Although the Switchblade works on the same basic principle as the Double Can-Can, it differs in that the degree of rotation in the rider's body is much more extreme. To sum it up, Metzger calls the move an inverted, twisted, upside-down Double Can-Can.

The trick starts off the same way as its predecessor, but by midflight, you'll notice, Metzger is looking almost behind him. At the same time, Metz swings his legs around wildly behind the bike, which really makes the trick unique. The higher and more spread apart his legs are, the better Metzger considers the extension.

To illustrate the trick, Mike Metzger—the inventor and the only rider who really does it to the extreme—is jumping a 70-foot gap at the Metal Mulisha compound in Lake Elsinore, California.

SWITCHBLADE

Mike Metzger
Lake Elsinore, California

Mike Metzger explains the
SWITCHBLADE

"The Switchblade is one of the coolest tricks I do, and is basically an extension of a standard Double Can-Can, but just takes it to a way farther extreme. The rider ends up looking almost completely backwards, with his feet and legs extended and almost upside down. To start the trick, I exit the lip and immediately take both feet off of the footpegs, getting ready to twist my hips and shoulders to the side of the bike right after the takeoff."

"You can see how quickly I get my feet up and over the seat, and I am careful not to catch them. I have thrown out my feet to the left side, as it is my preferred side to do Double Can-Cans. I get my legs out so fast because the quicker I get them out, the farther I can extend the trick."

"I am now twisting my whole body to the side. I start the twisting with my hips and legs, and continue on with turning my shoulders and head as well. Turning my head is a very important step to doing the trick well. To help my head around, I actually glance down at my feet as they spin to the side of the bike."

"In the fourth photo, I am almost fully extended towards the side of the bike. I continue to look back behind me, knowing that the farther I get my head around towards the back of the bike, the better extension I will get out of the Switchblade."

"This photo shows my full extension, and here you can see just how different this trick is compared to a regular Double Can-Can. My legs are completely inverted, and I am looking back towards the lip that I originally took off from."

"Again, you can see how influential my head movements are with this photo. The first thing I do when I have held the trick for a sufficient amount of time is bring back my head, almost looking directly towards the front fender already. At the same time, I begin twisting my hips and shoulders back towards the front as well. It is all one big motion."

"My shoulders are now fully balanced over my front end, and I am looking where I am going to land. I am bringing in my legs horizontally, so I don't catch the seat, and they end up almost in an Indian Air position. This happens because I am bringing my legs up so high past the seat."

8 "My left leg naturally drops a little quicker than my right, and by now it has almost found the footpeg. My right leg is clearing the seat with a couple of inches to spare, and I am staying nice and centered over the bike, with my head in a forward position."

9 "I have now spotted my landing, and I am still coming down from the elevation of the trick. I am also bringing my legs and feet towards their normal position on the pegs."

10 "In the last photo of the sequence, I have found my footpegs and I am in a normal position to land. I'm standing up with my knees and elbows slightly bent, ready to soak up the landing. I have plenty of time to ready myself for touching down, and I'm already thinking of what trick I'm going to do off the next hit!"

LAZY BOY

Resting on the job is not normally a part of the freestyle motocross competitor's schedule, but when seeing the **Lazy Boy,** you might wonder what the rider is doing kicking back in the air. In reality, he's not kicking back at all, he's performing one of the most difficult freestyle moves out there, one that leaves the freestyler in a straight-out, laid-back position on his bike.

The Lazy Boy is another move brought to the sport by teenage phenomenon Travis Pastrana. The Lazy Boy consists of the rider hitting a jump, and in midair laying his entire body back on the seat, completely horizontal. To complete the trick to its fullest extent, the rider brings his hands straight behind his head and extends them back. At the same time, his legs are kicked out, supporting the bike under the handlebars, with his head looking straight up toward the heavens. The stiffer and straighter the body is, the more impressed the judges will be.

Many of the professional riders can pull Lazy Boys, but some do it more frequently and a little more successfully than others. Riders who are most known for pulling the move during their routines are Kris Rourke, Clifford Adoptante, Adam Pierce, Travis Pastrana, and Kenny Bartram, although several other top guys can be seen pulling the Lazy Boy at contests.

Demonstrating the trick for us on the ensuing pages is Kris Rourke, who is riding at his personal track in Murrieta, California.

Mike Cinqmars
Providence, Rhode Island

LAZY BOY

93

Kris Rourke explains the
LAZY BOY

1 "In this first frame, I am just leaving the lip of the jump. I am in a normal 'attack' position, with my elbows out, my head looking forward, and my knees bent. You can see here that my left index finger is on my clutch. This technique allows me to make power or rpm adjustments to the bike to ensure that I will clear the jump smoothly and safely, and is a good idea to do on the face of any jump."

2 "Now I have left the face of the jump, and I am a few feet off the lip. I begin to throw the trick immediately. I have already eyed up the landing, and know that I have enough speed to make it, so I feel comfortable enough to begin the move. I almost look like I am in full 'squid mode' here, but the first step is to get my butt up towards the tank, while at the same time getting my upper body back more towards the rear fender."

"In the third shot, I begin to raise my feet up off of the pegs. I am also trying to focus on where I am going to put my knees on the bars. Some people set up for the trick differently, but I prefer to go as far forward as I can, to where I am almost sitting on the gas cap. My knees actually hit the bars here, and I wait until I feel this before going on to the next step."

"I now have my knees under the bars in the position where I want them. Some riders prefer to squeeze their knees against the fork tubes, but I don't. I like to just let them float out there because later on in the trick, when I am coming down, there is a chance that I could catch my legs on the radiator shrouds. Now that I have my legs under the bars, I direct my focus to my upper body. I have let go of the bars, and I'm bringing my torso back to lay it down on the seat and fender."

"This photo shows the full extension of my trick. The concentration here is on my legs, which I am trying to extend out as far and as straight as possible. I get my arms out as far as I can, trying to extend them out to make my body look as flat as it can. I also make sure that my head is looking straight up. In the air, I think about laying flat on the ground, and the position I would be in if I was doing that. This is the key to making the Lazy Boy realistic looking."

"I have now started to bring the trick back down. To accomplish this, I use a snapping motion where I hit my body on the seat to give it momentum to push me up towards the handlebars and back to a normal position. I begin to focus on where I will bring my hands when they reach the handlebars. I also try to get my body weight forward, because if it is too far back, the bike will begin to loop out."

"On this shot, I have my hands back on the grips where they should be. Once I have them on there, I can concentrate on getting my lower body back on to a comfortable position. I am trying to get my feet back onto the footpegs and get my body forward on the bike."

"I have my arms on the bars, but I am still trying to get my lower body back where it belongs, to a regular riding position. You can see that I have swung my legs down towards the pegs, but my upper body is still too far forward."

"In this final shot, I have finally made contact with my pegs. I have also brought my body back from sitting on the gas tank to a more normal position on the bike. I know now that I have successfully completed the jump, so now I am simply looking for my landing and trying to get comfortable before touching down on the dirt."

McMETZ

The list of insane new moves that Mike Metzger has contributed to the sport of freestyle motocross seems almost endless. Although many of the moves are based on similar tricks that have been done before, the McMetz is similar to many of Metzger's other patented tricks in that he also brought the original move to the sport.

The **McMetz** is one of the newest, most intense moves on the professional circuit, and Metzger is currently the only rider pulling off the trick, which is basically a Double Saran Wrap done with both feet. To do the McMetz, the rider must bring both feet up at the same time in a similar fashion to the Bar Hop. Once both boots are up and over the handlebars, the rider removes both hands simultaneously, freeing himself completely from the bike temporarily. While doing this, the rider swings both feet around the ends of the handlebars before returning them to the pegs and returning both hands to the grips.

Obviously, the McMetz is not the first trick for a beginner to practice. It takes years of freestyle riding to gain the kind of bike control that the trick requires. Riders who are considering trying the McMetz need to make sure that they can confidently pull Saran Wraps on both sides of their bikes with plenty of time to spare before attempting the move. The accompanying sequence features inventor Mike Metzger pulling the trick.

Mike Metzger
Lake Elsinore, California

McMETZ

Mike Metzger explains the
McMETZ

1 "The McMetz is a trick that I invented a while back that starts off with the rider basically just throwing a Bar Hop, and then it turns into a Double Saran Wrap, leaving the rider completely off of his bike for a split second. To start the trick, I am exiting the lip, really concentrating on keeping myself balanced and in a neutral position on the bike. If I leave the lip in an uncomfortable position, I won't even begin the McMetz, because it's just asking for trouble."

2 "Only 3 or 4 feet off of the lip, I already start to throw the trick by bringing my feet off of the footpegs. A key thing is to start the trick immediately after leaving the first hit so that the rider will have plenty of time later on to pull the trick."

3 "In the third photo, I have my knees completely tucked into my chest. I have to bring them really high up so I don't run the risk of catching my boots on the crossbar pad. I am also looking straight ahead, making sure that I get my heels and my feet completely over the front of my bike."

"Now I am almost in a Bar Hop position, but with my butt a little farther back than I would have it if I was doing a Bar Hop. I have my knees completely over the bars, trying to keep them nice and centered to maintain balance."

"In the fifth shot, I begin to spread my legs out. I am still concentrating on keeping my head centered, as this is one of the keys to keeping balanced. I am getting ready to let go with my hands, once I feel that I have spread out my legs far enough to allow a quick release of the bars."

6 "I am nice and centered at this point, and my head is looking down towards the bike and ground so I can see what I am doing. My legs are at a full spread-eagle, and I am bringing my arms back. To do this, I follow along my thighs, almost using them as a sort of guide to put my hands in the correct position."

7 "Bringing my legs completely around the handlebars, this is where the trick starts to resemble a Saran Wrap, but with both legs. Other than that, each leg is moved similarly to the trick. My hands are searching for the grips, and my body is still nice and balanced over the center of the bike."

McMETZ

"In the eighth shot, I have fortunately gotten my arms back down to the grips. Finding the grips is the scariest part of the trick, and it is a very comfortable feeling to finally find them and make contact with them. I'm still looking forward, and my feet are searching for the footpegs, which usually come pretty naturally."

"In the final photo, you can see that I am now securely back on my bike, with my hands on my grips and my feet on my pegs. I like to have a few feet to spare at the end of my trick, so that I can get back on the bike and fully brace my body for the landing. Remember, this trick is one of the harder ones, and takes some really quick reactions. The most important hint that I can express is to stay centered and balanced in the air."

INDIAN AIR
SUPERMAN
SEAT GRAB

Like so many of the freestyle tricks we see at contests, the **Indian Air Superman Seat Grab** has evolved over time and combines elements of several different tricks. As we mentioned before, the Superman was contributed to the sport by Supercross champ Jeremy McGrath. The trick was then stepped up by Carey Hart, who added the "seat grab" part.

From there, the trick's development continued when riders added the sideways scissors kick, or Indian Air portion. Riders like Mike Metzger and Tommy Clowers pioneered Indian Airs, with Metzger doing them out to the side of his bike during Double Can-Cans and Clowers doing them over the top of his seat.

The combination of all of these tricks adds up to one awe-inspiring move: the Indian Air Superman Seat Grab. The first step in doing this fairly complicated move is to throw out a regular Superman Seat Grab, but once extension is reached, the rider turns sideways, throws his feet out, and does what resembles a scissors kick. Several top riders do the trick, but the ones most noted for it are long-legged teenage sensation Travis Pastrana and Metal Mulisha rider Brian Deegan, both of whom throw the move out to its fullest extent regularly during contests. Deegan demonstrates here.

Clifford Adoptante
Arrowhead Pond

Brian Deegan explains the

INDIAN AIR
SUPERMAN
SEAT GRAB

1 "This trick is pretty difficult, so riders need to make sure that they are doing regular Superman Seat Grabs relatively easily before attempting the move. I approach the takeoff for the Indian Air Superman Seat Grab similar to the way that I approach the other Superman Seat Grab tricks I do, like the Hart Attack. Immediately off of the lip, maybe 2 or 3 feet into the air, I am already beginning to bring my left hand back, taking it off of the grip before I even do anything with my legs."

2 "I always wait until I have a nice, firm grasp on my left-hand-side grab handle that is cut into my side number plate before I do anything else. Once I feel that I have a good hold onto the frame, the next step in the trick is to remove my feet from the footpegs. With my feet off the pegs, I start to bring my legs back towards the rear fender."

"In this third photo, I am beginning to bring my whole entire body back towards the rear of the bike. I haven't gotten into the horizontal Superman Seat Grab position yet, as I am still gaining altitude and bringing my body back. My head is in an upwards, forward position, and I am double-checking to make sure that I will clear the jump clearly before I commit to doing the trick."

"This is the point where I would normally throw my legs straight back for a Superman Seat Grab, but since I am doing the Indian Air variation, I instead start to turn my body to the left. This should be done by turning my hips first, which will allow the rest of my body to twist around accordingly."

"In this picture, my full extension is captured. You can see here that my hips are twisted completely to the left, at a 90-degree angle to the ground. This is where the Indian Air really comes in, and you can see how much different the trick looks compared to a regular Superman Seat Grab. My legs are captured doing their 'scissors' motion, with my right leg kicking out to the front and my left leg kicking out to the rear."

"After throwing out the trick as far as I can, I begin my descent back down towards the ground. To start this portion, the first thing I do is stabilize my body, bringing it back to a normal, horizontal position on the bike. Once I am straightened out and I feel comfortable with the way my body is suspended, I can start to bring the trick back to a normal position."

"In one swift move, I am throwing my body weight up to the front of the bike. I do this by taking my left hand off of the grab handle, which automatically returns to the grips. At the same time, I bring my legs and feet up towards the footpegs and pull my weight up to the front, using both the boost I received from the grab handle, as well as pulling myself up with my right hand."

"Now that my legs have found the pegs and my hands have found the grips, I am basically in cruise control. I have also spotted my landing, and I know that I have plenty of time to straighten out the front end and prepare myself for landing. As with any trick, I want to land smoothly. To do this, I keep standing and use my legs and elbows as shock absorbers."

Of all the tricks that modern freestyle athletes are doing, the **Cordova** is arguably the most impressive, and one of the most difficult. Cordovas were brought to us by one of the most talented freestyle riders out there. European freestyler Edgar Torronteras started pulling the move during various contests and halftime exhibitions at Supercross races overseas, and it was an immediate success.

Performing the back-bending maneuver takes some serious flexibility on the rider's part, not to mention nerves of steel. Once in the air, the Cordova is completed by the rider hooking both feet under the handlebars, leaving both hands on the grips, and bending his back in an arch.

At peak extension, the rider's head is completely upside down and looking directly backward, toward the takeoff of the jump. To pull the trick really well, some riders will actually place their helmet's visor on the rear of the seat, leaving their backs completely arched out, and also leaving the riders blind and oblivious to what is going on in front of them.

Several top riders incorporate the Cordova into their run, including guys like Brian Deegan, Clifford Adoptante, Justin Homan, Edgar Torronteras, and Ronnie Faisst. Demonstrating the Cordova on the following pages is Ronnie Faisst, who has taken the trick to a new level, due to his unbelievable flexibility.

CORDOVA

Ronnie Faisst
Providence, Rhode Island

Ronnie Faisst explains the
CORDOVA

"**The Cordova** is one of the most difficult tricks out there because it feels so awkward, and the rider's sense of balance gets thrown off easily. It is hard for a rider to see what he is doing, and everything happens very fast, so riders need to be careful on their first few attempts. I approach the lip with my body leaning just slightly farther forward than normal to keep the front end from going up too far, and I am in a standing position."

"After I am a few feet in the air and I feel like I took off correctly, I start the trick. The first thing I do is bring my feet up towards the handlebars in preparation to hook them under the bars. As you can see from the photo, I keep the bike as level as possible in the air."

"Now that the bike is leveled up, I commit to the trick by bringing my feet all the way to the bars and hooking them under. This part of the trick is very similar to the setup for a Cliffhanger."

"Here, the trick starts to differ from the Cliffhanger. I push my knees out and I push my hips up. At the same time, I begin to bring my head back and try to think about doing a back bend. The most important part here is to get my knees out in front of the handlebars as far as they will go."

5 "At this point, I'm thinking about getting full extension out of my back and body. The secret to doing this is the use of my knees. If I do it right, my knees will give me increased leverage and let me tweak the trick out more. Also, if I pull hard with my arms, my head will go back even farther. I should be looking directly back, and if possible, touch my helmet's visor to the seat."

6 "As soon as I feel my bike start to drop from the maximum height of the jump, I immediately start to bring my head back to a level position and try to orient myself to my position in the air. I don't really worry about my legs yet. I just want to make sure that my head is back to a normal position."

"Once I have my upper body under control, my legs seem to come down naturally and effortlessly. I find the pegs with my feet and prepare for landing in a neutral, comfortable position. Since I am almost sitting on the seat on the way down anyway, I can feel the seat hit my butt."

"The last step is the landing, and if a rider follows the rest of the steps, it should come fairly easy. Because I am in a sitting position when coming down from the Cordova, I need to stand back up on the pegs to absorb the shock of landing."

PHOTO GALLERY

Travis Pastrana
Rodeo
Providence,
Rhode Island

Larry Linkogle
Superman
Lake Elsinore,
California

Kris Rourke interviewed by Cameron Steele, Costa Mesa, California

Mike Metzger
Stalefish Saran Wrap
Lake Elsinore, California

Brian Deegan
Hart Attack
Lake Elsinore, California

Carey Hart, *Nothing*, Providence, Rhode Island

Kris Rourke, *Whip*, Irwindale Speedway

Ronnie Faisst
Costa Mesa, California

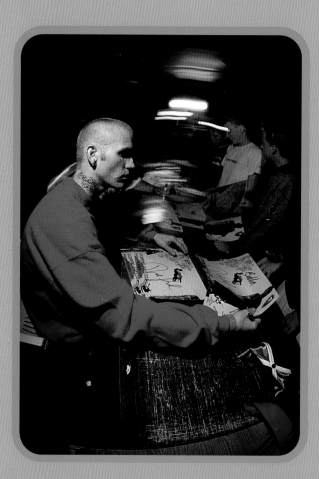

Travis Pastrana
Whipped Superman
Seat Grab
Providence,
Rhode Island

Mike Metzger, *No-Footed Whip***, Lake Elsinore, California**

Brian Deegan
Mulisha Grab
**Providence,
Rhode Island**

Clifford Adoptante, *Stalefish Saran Wrap*
Perris, California

Kenny Bartram
Faceplant!
Providence, Rhode Island

Carey Hart
Cliffhanger
Lake Elsinore, California

Brian Deegan, Mike
Metzger, and Ronnie Faisst
Lake Elsinore, California

Travis Pastrana, *Heel Clicker*

Providence, Rhode Island

Reagan Sieg, *Indian Air Superman Seat Grab*

Murrieta, California

Brian Deegan, *Superman Seat Grab*, **Providence, Rhode Island**

Travis Pastrana and Kenny Bartram
Double Can-Can, No-Footed Whip
Providence, Rhode Island

INDEX